Wyoming Bingo Book

COMPLETE BINGO GAME IN A BOOK

Written By Rebecca Stark
Educational Books 'n' Bingo

Educational Books 'n' Bingo

ISBN 978-0-87386-543-2

Printed in the U.S.A.

DIRECTIONS

INCLUDED:

List of Terms

Templates for Additional Terms and Clues

2 Clues per Term

30 Unique Bingo Cards

Markers

1. **Either cut apart the book or make copies of ALL the sheets. You might want to make an extra copy of the clue sheets to use for introduction and review. Keep the sheets in an envelope for easy reuse.**

2. Cut apart the call cards with terms and clues.

3. Pass out one bingo card per student. There are enough for a class of 30.

4. Pass out markers. You may cut apart the markers included in this book or use any other small items of your choice.

5. Decide whether or not you will require the entire card to be filled. Requiring the entire card to be filled provides a better review. However, if you have a short time to fill, you may prefer to have them do the just the border or some other format. Tell the class before you begin what is required.

6. There are 50 terms. Read the list before you begin. If there are any terms that have not been covered in class, you may want to read to the students the term and clues before you begin.

7. There is a blank space in the middle of each card. You can instruct the students to use it as a free space or you can write in answers to cover terms not included. Of course, in this case you would create your own clues. (Templates provided.)

8. Shuffle the cards and place them in a pile. Two or three clues are provided for each term. If you plan to play the game with the same group more than once, you might want to choose a different clue for each game. If not, you may choose to use more than one clue.

9. Be sure to keep the cards you have used for the present game in a separate pile. When a student calls, "Bingo," he or she will have to verify that the correct answers are on his or her card AND that the markers were placed in response to the proper questions. Pull out the cards that are on the student's card keeping them in the order they were used in the game. Read each clue as it was given and ask the student to identify the correct answer from his or her card.

10. If the student has the correct answers on the card AND has shown that they were marked in response to the *correct questions,* then that student is the winner and the game is over. If the student does not have the correct answers on the card OR he or she marked the answers in response to *the wrong questions,* then the game continues until there is a proper winner.

11. If you want to play again, reshuffle the cards and begin again.

Have fun!

TERMS INCLUDED

Bison

Border(-ed)

Bridger

Casper

Cheyenne

Climate

Code

William F. Cody

Continental Divide

Cottonwood(s)

Counties

Cowboy

Crazy Horse

Crop(s)

Cutthroat Trout

Devil's Tower

Equality State

Executive Branch

Flag

Fort Laramie

Gannett Peak

Great Plains

Horned Lizard

Intermontane Basins

Jade

Judicial Branch

Knightia

Lake(s)

Legislative Branch

Livestock

Meadowlark

Mining (-ed)

Esther Hobart Morris

Oregon Trail

Plateau

Pony Express

Rivers

Rocky Mountains

Rodeo

Sacajawea

Seal

Shoshone National Forest

Teton

Tribes

Triceratops

Union

Western Wheatgrass

"Wyoming"

Wyoming Territory

Yellowstone

Wyoming Bingo

Additional Terms

Choose as many additional terms as you would like and write them in the squares. Repeat each as desired.
Cut out the squares and randomly distribute them to the class.
Instruct the students to place their square on the center space of their card.

Clues for Additional Terms

Write two clues for each of your additional terms.

_____ 1. 2.	_____ 1. 2.
_____ 1. 2.	_____ 1. 2. .
_____ 1. 2.	_____ 1. 2.

© **Barbara M. Peller**

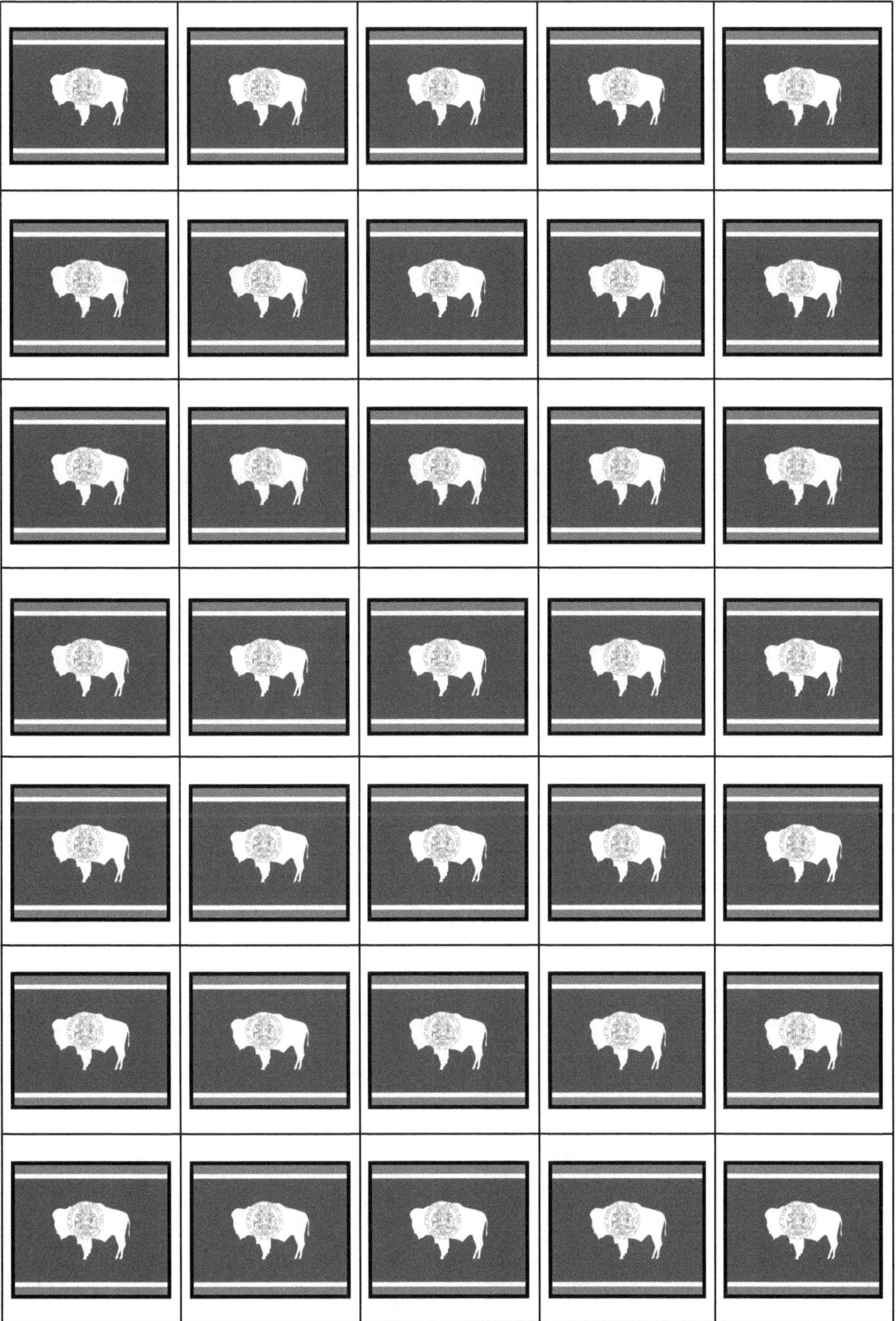

Bison 1. The ___, the largest land animal in North America, is the state mammal. 2. At one time millions of ___ roamed the Great Plains in herds.	**Border(-ed)** 1. Wyoming is ___ by Montana, Utah, Colorado, South Dakota, Nebraska, Idaho, and Utah. 2. Yellowstone National Park forms part of the ___ of three states: Wyoming, Idaho, and Montana.
Bridger 1. Jim ___ was a mountain man, trapper, fur trader, scout, and guide. He was an important guide for the U.S. Army in the mid-1850s. 2. In 1843 Jim ___ established a fort in southwestern Wyoming. Like Fort Laramie, Fort ___ was an important way station for emigrants traveling westward on the Oregon Trail.	**Casper** 1. ___ is the second largest city in Wyoming. 2. ___ is in east-central Wyoming along the North Platte River. The nearby Fort ___ is now a National Historic Site.
Cheyenne 1. ___ is the capital of Wyoming. 2. ___ is the largest city in Wyoming. The next two largest are Casper and Laramie.	**Climate** 1. Wyoming has a semiarid ___. 2. Because of its elevation, Wyoming has a relatively cool ___.
Code 1. The state ___ of Wyoming was derived from *Cowboy Ethics,* by James P. Owen. 2. The first line of the state ___ is "Live each day with courage." The last is "Know where to draw the line."	**William F. Cody** 1. ___'s nickname was "Buffalo Bill." A city in Park County is named for him. 2. This frontiersman and entertainer is best known for his Wild West Show.
Continental Divide 1. The ___ crosses into Wyoming within Yellowstone National Park and continues southeast into Colorado. 2. In the United States, rivers east of the ___ flow into the Atlantic Ocean. Those west of the ___ flow into Pacific Ocean.	**Cottonwood(s)** 1. The plains ___ is the state tree. 2. ___ are named for the cottonlike mass of hairs surrounding their seeds. The plains ___ has hairy buds and light yellow branchlets.

Wyoming Bingo

Counties	**Cowboy**
1. There are 23 ___ in Wyoming. 2. The original 5 ___ are Laramie; Carter, which was renamed Sweetwater; Carbon; Albany; and Uinta.	1. Wyoming officially adopted a ___ on a bucking horse as a symbol of the state. 2. A ___ on a bucking horse is on the state quarter.
Crazy Horse	**Crop(s)**
1. ___ was a Native American war leader of the Oglala Lakota. 2. He was a fierce warrior, determined to preserve the Lakota people's traditional way of life.	1. Hay is the most important ___. It is used to feed the cattle, by far the most important agricultural product in the state. 2. Hay, sugar beets, barley, dry beans, and wheat are the state's top five ___.
Cutthroat Trout	**Devil's Tower**
1. The ___ is the state fish. It is named for the orange mark behind its lower jaw. 2. The ___ is a species of freshwater fish in the salmon family.	1. ___ rises out of the prairie in the Black Hills. It is sacred to the Lakota and other tribes. 2. President Theodore Roosevelt declared ___ a national monument in 1906. It was the first national monument.
Equality State	**Executive Branch**
1. Wyoming is known as the ___ and the Cowboy State. 2. The nickname ___ came about because Wyoming was the first state to specifically give women the right to vote.	1. The ___ of government enacts and enforces the laws. The ___ comprises the governor, secretary of state, auditor, treasurer, and superintendent of public education. 2. The governor is head of the ___. The present-day governor is [fill in].
Flag	**Fort Laramie**
1. The state ___ is red, white, and blue. Its blue field is surrounded by a red and white border. A white bison is centered on the field. 2. The Great Seal of Wyoming is depicted on the bison on the state ___.	1. Established in 1834 as a fur-trading fort, ___ was the first permanent trading post in Wyoming. It later became the largest military post on the Northern Plains. 2. ___ was an important outpost on the Oregon Trail system. It became a link in the Pony Express, the Overland Stage Line, and the transcontinental telegraph systems.

Wyoming Bingo

Gannett Peak	**Great Plains**
1. At 13,804 feet, ___ is the highest point in the state. It is in the Wind River Range, part of the Rocky Mountains. 2. Complete this analogy: Belle Fourche River : lowest point :: ___ : highest point	1. The ___ lie east of the Rocky Mountains; the area is characterized by short-grass prairie. 2. The ___ spread into the northeast corner of Wyoming from South Dakota. Though primarily composed of grassland, the Black Hills region features forested hills, canyons, buttes, rivers and reservoirs.
Horned Lizard	**Intermontane* Basins**
1. The ___ is the state reptile. Because of its short, blunt snout, it is sometimes mistakingly called a toad. 2. When a ___ feels threatened, it flattens and freezes in place, trying to blend with the ground.	1. The relatively flat areas between the state's mountain ranges are part of the ___. They are covered by short grasses and lower brush. 2. The ___ include the Bighorn River, Powder River, Wind River, Green River, Great Divide, and Washakie basins. *Intermontane = the "land between the mountains."
Jade	**Judicial Branch**
1. ___ is the state gemstone. 2. ___ can be cut from the minerals jadeite or nephrite. Wyoming's state gemstone is cut from nephrite.	1. The ___ interprets what our laws mean and makes decisions about the laws and those who break them. 2. The Supreme Court is the highest court in the ___ of the state government.
Knightia	**Lake(s)**
1. ___ is the state fossil. 2. ___ is an extinct genus of fish. Abundant ___ fossils have been found in the state's Green River Formation.	1. There are many ___ in the Grand Teton National Park. Most were formed by glaciers. An example is Jackson ___. 2. Yellowstone ___ in Yellowstone National Park is the largest body of water in Wyoming.
Legislative Branch	**Livestock**
1. The ___ of government comprises the Senate and the House of Representatives. 2. The ___ makes the laws.	1. More than 85% of the state's agricultural receipts are from ___ products. 2. The most important ___ products are beef cattle and calves. Hogs, and sheep and lambs are also important.

Meadowlark	**Mining (-ed)**
1. The western ___ is the state bird. 2. The western ___ is in the same family as blackbirds and orioles.	1. ___ is an important industry in Wyoming. The state is the leading producer of coal and a leader in the production of petroleum and natural gas. 2. Coal, petroleum, and natural gas are the most important ___ products.
Esther Hobart Morris	**Oregon Trail**
1. ___ was a pioneer for women's suffrage. 2. ___ was appointed the nation's first female justice of the peace in 1870. She filled the term of James W. Stillman, who resigned after the Wyoming Territory passed an equality bill.	1. The ___ is an east-west wagon route and emigrant trail that connected the Missouri River to valleys in Oregon and locations in between. 2. Independence Rock, 50 miles southwest of Casper, was a landmark on the ___.
Plateau	**Pony Express**
1. Wyoming is basically a large ___ broken by several high mountain ranges. 2. A ___ is an extensive land area having a relatively level surface raised sharply above adjacent land on at least one side.	1. This fast mail service used mounted riders instead of traditional stagecoaches. 2. Fort Bridger, Granger, South Pass, Split Rock, Devil's Gate, Independence Rock, Red Buttes, Casper, and Fort Laramie were ___ stations.
Rivers	**Rocky Mountains**
1. The Snake, Wind/Bighorn, Yellowstone, Green, and North Platte are the largest ___ in Wyoming. 2. The Belle Fourche ___ is the lowest point in the state at 3,099 feet above sea level. It flows past Devil's Tower.	1. The Laramie Mountains, the Wind River Range and the Big Horn Mountains are all part of this major mountain range. 2. Gannett Peak, the highest point in Wyoming, is found in the Wind River Range, which is part of this mountain range.
Rodeo	**Sacajawea**
1. ___ is the state sport. Riders display their skill in activities related to the raising of livestock. 2. The term ___ comes from the Spanish word *rodear,* meaning "to surround." It originally meant "roundup."	1. ___ was the Shoshone Indian who assisted the Lewis and Clark expedition. 2. The ___ golden dollar coin is the state coin.

Wyoming Bingo

Seal 1. The state's motto, "Equal Rights," is on the Great ___ of the State of Wyoming. 2. The two men on the Great ___ represent the mining and livestock industries.	**Shoshone National Forest** 1. The ___ was the first federally protected National Forest in the United States. 2. The ___ was set aside in 1891 as part of the Yellowstone Timberland Reserve.
Teton 1. The ___ Mountains tower over a mile above Jackson Hole Valley. Grand ___ National Park is named for the tallest mountain in that range. 2. Grand ___ National Park in northwestern Wyoming includes most of the northern part of the valley known as Jackson Hole.	**Tribes** 1. The Arapaho, Cheyenne, Crow, Shoshone, and Ute ___ were original inhabitants of what is now Wyoming. 2. Today there are two federally recognized Indian ___ in Wyoming: the Shoshone and the Arapaho tribes. They share a single reservation.
Triceratops 1. ___ is the state dinosaur. There is also a state fossil, *Knightia,* an extinct fish. 2. ___ had three horns on its skull: one on its snout and one above each eye.	**Union** 1. Wyoming was admitted to the ___ on July 10, 1890. 2. Wyoming was the 44th state to be admitted to the ___.
Western Wheatgrass 1. ___ is the state grass. 2. This tough native prairie grass provides hay and pasture for both wild and domestic animals.	**"Wyoming"** 1. ___ is the state song. 2. ___ begins, "In the far and mighty West, where the crimson sun seeks rest."
Wyoming Territory 1. ___ was carved from sections of Dakota, Utah, and Idaho territories, 2. The first governor of ___, John A. Campbell, was appointed by President Ulysses S. Grant in 1869.	**Yellowstone** 1. ___ was the world's first national park. About 96 % of it lies in Wyoming. 2. ___ National Park is best known for Old Faithful and its other geysers. It also has one of the world's largest petrified forests and more than 290 waterfalls.

Wyoming Bingo

Wyoming Bingo

Rocky Mountains	Bison	Bridger	Executive Branch	Livestock
Devil's Tower	Border(-ed)	"Wyoming"	Legislative Branch	Seal
Western Wheatgrass	Lake(s)		Plateau	Wyoming Territory
Union	Sacajawea	Triceratops	Knightia	Mining (-ed)
Oregon Trail	Gannett Peak	Crazy Horse	Teton	Intermontane Basins

Wyoming Bingo

Union	Western Wheatgrass	Horned Lizard	Rodeo	Judicial Branch
Mining (-ed)	Crop(s)	Code	Sacajawea	Esther Hobart Morris
Continental Divide	Gannett Peak		Great Plains	Triceratops
Pony Express	Rivers	Lake(s)	Yellowstone	Livestock
Seal	"Wyoming"	Crazy Horse	Devil's Tower	Teton

Wyoming Bingo

Gannett Peak	Triceratops	Crop(s)	Knightia	Western Wheatgrass
Mining (-ed)	Border(-ed)	William F. Cody	Bison	Fort Laramie
Sacajawea	"Wyoming"		Esther Hobart Morris	Casper
Lake(s)	Continental Divide	Oregon Trail	Pony Express	Horned Lizard
Teton	Cottonwood(s)	Crazy Horse	Yellowstone	Judicial Branch

Wyoming Bingo

Lake(s)	Esther Hobart Morris	Bridger	Cottonwood(s)	Judicial Branch
Meadowlark	Climate	Bison	Rodeo	Western Wheatgrass
Plateau	Pony Express		Intermontane Basins	Executive Branch
Triceratops	Border(-ed)	"Wyoming"	Crazy Horse	Code
Counties	Seal	Cheyenne	Teton	Wyoming Territory

Wyoming Bingo

Seal	Livestock	Sacajawea	Code	Cottonwood(s)
Meadowlark	Triceratops	William F. Cody	Great Plains	Border(-ed)
Bridger	Wyoming Territory		Legislative Branch	Flag
Intermontane Basins	Judicial Branch	Rocky Mountains	Yellowstone	Cowboy
Crop(s)	Crazy Horse	Western Wheatgrass	Lake(s)	Plateau

Wyoming Bingo: Card No. 5

Wyoming Bingo

Casper	Esther Hobart Morris	Horned Lizard	Judicial Branch	Wyoming Territory
Knightia	Sacajawea	Cowboy	Bison	Western Wheatgrass
Rodeo	Counties		Climate	Great Plains
Crazy Horse	Oregon Trail	Yellowstone	Cheyenne	Bridger
Mining (-ed)	Code	Rocky Mountains	Plateau	Cutthroat Trout

Wyoming Bingo

Rocky Mountains	Esther Hobart Morris	Flag	Triceratops	Crop(s)
Mining (-ed)	Judicial Branch	Gannett Peak	Border(-ed)	Meadowlark
Wyoming Territory	Executive Branch		Great Plains	Climate
Lake(s)	Pony Express	William F. Cody	Union	Continental Divide
Crazy Horse	Cottonwood(s)	Yellowstone	Cheyenne	Casper

Wyoming Bingo

Plateau	Esther Hobart Morris	Equality State	Knightia	Climate
Meadowlark	Bridger	Rodeo	Wyoming Territory	Code
Cutthroat Trout	Cottonwood(s)		Judicial Branch	Livestock
Teton	Lake(s)	Union	Counties	Pony Express
"Wyoming"	Crazy Horse	Cheyenne	Sacajawea	Mining (-ed)

Wyoming Bingo: Card No. 8

Wyoming Bingo

Great Plains	Crop(s)	Gannett Peak	Cutthroat Trout	Cottonwood(s)
Counties	Judicial Branch	Plateau	Sacajawea	Esther Hobart Morris
Fort Laramie	Rocky Mountains		Border(-ed)	Equality State
Cowboy	Livestock	Oregon Trail	Legislative Branch	Flag
Pony Express	Yellowstone	William F. Cody	Union	Intermontane Basins

Wyoming Bingo: Card No. 9

Wyoming Bingo

Union	Knightia	Climate	Rodeo	Cutthroat Trout
Wyoming Territory	Code	Bison	Border(-ed)	Judicial Branch
Cottonwood(s)	Esther Hobart Morris		Executive Branch	Continental Divide
Oregon Trail	Intermontane Basins	Cowboy	Yellowstone	Fort Laramie
William F. Cody	Mining (-ed)	Horned Lizard	Seal	Plateau

Wyoming Bingo: Card No. 10

Wyoming Bingo

Casper	Esther Hobart Morris	Sacajawea	Cowboy	Mining (-ed)
Equality State	Fort Laramie	Legislative Branch	Great Plains	Bison
Meadowlark	Judicial Branch		Horned Lizard	Gannett Peak
William F. Cody	Western Wheatgrass	Yellowstone	Cottonwood(s)	Union
Counties	Crazy Horse	Rocky Mountains	Cheyenne	Crop(s)

Wyoming Bingo: Card No. 11

Wyoming Bingo

Crop(s)	Livestock	Fort Laramie	Knightia	Great Plains
Gannett Peak	Mining (-ed)	Bridger	Cheyenne	Border(-ed)
Rocky Mountains	Flag		Wyoming Territory	Rodeo
Crazy Horse	Pony Express	Judicial Branch	Union	Meadowlark
Esther Hobart Morris	Equality State	Cottonwood(s)	Counties	Code

Wyoming Bingo

Cowboy	Livestock	Casper	Fort Laramie	Wyoming Territory
Bridger	Equality State	Judicial Branch	Great Plains	Continental Divide
Knightia	Code		Gannett Peak	Flag
Plateau	Yellowstone	Climate	Cottonwood(s)	Union
Crazy Horse	Intermontane Basins	Cheyenne	Rocky Mountains	Legislative Branch

Wyoming Bingo: Card No. 13

Wyoming Bingo

Devil's Tower	Judicial Branch	Sacajawea	Great Plains	Counties
Code	Rocky Mountains	Fort Laramie	Border(-ed)	Esther Hobart Morris
Cowboy	Executive Branch		Horned Lizard	William F. Cody
Intermontane Basins	Yellowstone	Cottonwood(s)	Climate	Casper
Crazy Horse	Rodeo	Continental Divide	Mining (-ed)	Plateau

Wyoming Bingo: Card No. 14

Wyoming Bingo

Legislative Branch	Great Plains	Sacajawea	Crop(s)	Knightia
Casper	Horned Lizard	Bison	Bridger	Counties
Wyoming Territory	Rocky Mountains		Western Wheatgrass	Esther Hobart Morris
Crazy Horse	Fort Laramie	Equality State	Yellowstone	Cowboy
Mining (-ed)	Pony Express	Cheyenne	Cutthroat Trout	Gannett Peak

Wyoming Bingo: Card No. 15

Wyoming Bingo

Climate	Fort Laramie	Equality State	Cutthroat Trout	Rivers
Rodeo	Continental Divide	Flag	Meadowlark	Executive Branch
Cowboy	Livestock		Wyoming Territory	Gannett Peak
Lake(s)	Code	Crazy Horse	Legislative Branch	Union
Counties	Tribes	Cheyenne	Pony Express	Esther Hobart Morris

Wyoming Bingo: Card No. 16

Wyoming Bingo

William F. Cody	Shoshone National Forest	Jade	Fort Laramie	Devil's Tower
Legislative Branch	Counties	Yellowstone	Executive Branch	Flag
Great Plains	Plateau		Tribes	Equality State
Intermontane Basins	Mining (-ed)	Union	Sacajawea	Continental Divide
Oregon Trail	Cowboy	Crop(s)	Knightia	Livestock

Wyoming Bingo

Cutthroat Trout	Cottonwood(s)	Code	Cowboy	Rodeo
Esther Hobart Morris	William F. Cody	Oregon Trail	Wyoming Territory	Counties
Great Plains	Continental Divide		Jade	Bridger
Livestock	Bison	Yellowstone	Union	Horned Lizard
Tribes	Fort Laramie	Sacajawea	Shoshone National Forest	Casper

Wyoming Bingo: Card No. 18

Wyoming Bingo

Wyoming Territory	**Casper**	**Fort Laramie**	**Equality State**	**Union**
Legislative Branch	**Knightia**	**Esther Hobart Morris**	**Crop(s)**	**Executive Branch**
Shoshone National Forest	Cottonwood(s)		**Border(-ed)**	**Western Wheatgrass**
Horned Lizard	**Tribes**	**Oregon Trail**	**Pony Express**	**Jade**
Bridger	**Rivers**	**Mining (-ed)**	**Plateau**	**Cheyenne**

Wyoming Bingo: Card No. 19

Wyoming Bingo

Devil's Tower	Shoshone National Forest	Knightia	Fort Laramie	Cheyenne
Code	Gannett Peak	Meadowlark	Oregon Trail	Rodeo
Livestock	Flag		Lake(s)	Bison
Seal	"Wyoming"	Teton	Pony Express	Tribes
Triceratops	Plateau	Rivers	Union	Jade

Wyoming Bingo

Legislative Branch	Casper	Meadowlark	Fort Laramie	Seal
Livestock	Jade	Climate	Equality State	Rocky Mountains
Continental Divide	Mining (-ed)		Shoshone National Forest	Sacajawea
Oregon Trail	Crop(s)	Tribes	Intermontane Basins	Plateau
Lake(s)	Rivers	Cheyenne	William F. Cody	Pony Express

Wyoming Bingo: Card No. 21

Wyoming Bingo

Cutthroat Trout	Horned Lizard	Jade	Bridger	Cowboy
Rodeo	Knightia	Western Wheatgrass	Equality State	Border(-ed)
Code	Executive Branch		Rocky Mountains	Flag
Tribes	Intermontane Basins	Pony Express	Bison	Meadowlark
Rivers	William F. Cody	Shoshone National Forest	Continental Divide	Lake(s)

Wyoming Bingo: Card No. 22

© Barbara M. Peller

Wyoming Bingo

Climate	Shoshone National Forest	Crop(s)	Bridger	Cheyenne
Casper	Devil's Tower	Mining (-ed)	Legislative Branch	Bison
Horned Lizard	Cowboy		Teton	Rocky Mountains
Continental Divide	Rivers	Tribes	William F. Cody	Pony Express
Seal	"Wyoming"	Plateau	Oregon Trail	Jade

Wyoming Bingo

Climate	Plateau	Devil's Tower	Shoshone National Forest	Equality State
Jade	Cheyenne	Meadowlark	Rodeo	Rocky Mountains
Flag	Cutthroat Trout		Cowboy	Continental Divide
Seal	Teton	Tribes	William F. Cody	Livestock
Triceratops	Lake(s)	Rivers	Knightia	"Wyoming"

Wyoming Bingo

Lake(s)	Meadowlark	Shoshone National Forest	Sacajawea	Jade
Bison	Livestock	Legislative Branch	Climate	Border(-ed)
Intermontane Basins	Equality State		Teton	Tribes
Western Wheatgrass	Seal	"Wyoming"	Rivers	Executive Branch
Cheyenne	Devil's Tower	Code	Counties	Triceratops

Wyoming Bingo: Card No. 25

Wyoming Bingo

Jade	Shoshone National Forest	Horned Lizard	Rodeo	Cutthroat Trout
Oregon Trail	Knightia	Equality State	Devil's Tower	Climate
Intermontane Basins	Teton		Executive Branch	Lake(s)
William F. Cody	Bridger	Seal	Rivers	Tribes
Flag	Counties	Sacajawea	"Wyoming"	Triceratops

Wyoming Bingo

Horned Lizard	Code	Shoshone National Forest	Devil's Tower	Gannett Peak
Seal	Teton	Legislative Branch	Tribes	Border(-ed)
Yellowstone	"Wyoming"		Rivers	Lake(s)
Cutthroat Trout	Casper	Meadowlark	Triceratops	Bison
Counties	Executive Branch	Jade	Western Wheatgrass	Flag

Wyoming Bingo: Card No. 27

Wyoming Bingo

Horned Lizard	Devil's Tower	Western Wheatgrass	Shoshone National Forest	Climate
Gannett Peak	Jade	Teton	Rodeo	Executive Branch
"Wyoming"	Continental Divide		Flag	Oregon Trail
Union	Cutthroat Trout	Mining (-ed)	Rivers	Tribes
Bridger	Great Plains	Counties	Triceratops	Seal

Wyoming Bingo: Card No. 28

Wyoming Bingo

Jade	Devil's Tower	Cutthroat Trout	Legislative Branch	Great Plains
Pony Express	Oregon Trail	Meadowlark	Flag	Western Wheatgrass
Intermontane Basins	Teton		Border(-ed)	Shoshone National Forest
Gannett Peak	Seal	Judicial Branch	Rivers	Tribes
Climate	Equality State	Triceratops	Casper	"Wyoming"

Wyoming Bingo: Card No. 29

Wyoming Bingo

Cottonwood(s)	Shoshone National Forest	Rodeo	Great Plains	Tribes
Bison	Devil's Tower	Horned Lizard	Executive Branch	Border(-ed)
Intermontane Basins	Cowboy		Flag	Meadowlark
Triceratops	Casper	Bridger	Rivers	Teton
Seal	Wyoming Territory	"Wyoming"	Jade	Western Wheatgrass

Wyoming Bingo: Card No. 30